Yet Will I Serve Him

Some names have been removed
to protect the guilty

Author – Kimberly Stratton
Publisher – The Crown And Cross Publishing Co LLC
Cover – Antonio Vance

Kimberly Stratton
International H.O.P.E. Inc.
PO Box 952607
Lake Mary, FL 32795
ISBN: 9798703509272

Intentionally blank page

My life: family, friends, love, lies, sexual relationships, alcohol, life lessons, church leadership, ministry, church hurt and everything between. Do you remember every single detail of your life from the second you were born? Neither can I; however, I will give you the graphic truth and detailed highlights. After running from God for 12 years, I was tired of myself and the life I was living. Feeling the call of God (the aching hole in my heart), I finally surrendered and returned to church in late October 2010. In November of 2010, I rededicated my life back to Christ. In December of 2010, I joined a church and never looked back on my relationship with God ~ not once. Through the trials, tribulations, backstabbing, tears, fears and trying to remove the noise from others as well as myself from inside of my head, I faithfully served God. I was talked about across the pulpit, used, experienced jealousy from saints of God including church leadership; saints told by church leaders to no longer interact with me when God released me from their ministry, attempted to be manipulated by ministries and at times shunned; sexually propositioned by a Pastor and a Deacon, a handful of saints who physically jumped up in my face and still I pressed on. I stood up for what was right when money was being stolen from God's House. I knew God's plan was and still is greater than mine. I had good and not so good people come into my life. They all served their purpose as God ordained. When man tried to do evil in my life, God turned it around for His good. No matter what, I made a vow that *Yet Will I Serve Him*.

Dedication

I dedicate this book to life, its experiences (the good and not so good) and its lessons that have shaped me; which allowed God to mold me. In this process, I thank God that no matter what I have been through, He gave me the heart to survive, forgive and press forward.

Even though I cannot share EVERY little detail of my life that I have been through, this book details the highlights.

These events from my life outlined in this autobiography are based on what I have seen, heard and experienced. I will not name names or companies to protect the guilty ones.

Intentionally blank page

Table of Contents

Lessons – Part 1

Family

Friends

Love

Lessons – Part 2

Prologue

I am not sure who the original author is but

there is a song that says "when I look back over my life and I think things over, I can truly say that I've been blessed. I've got a testimony". We never really know how BLESSED we are. As humans we forget but God never forgets. Therefore, the Holy Spirit has to bring things back to our remembrance (and various social media platforms sharing our prior victories and memories help also).

God has brought me so far. I remember, when I was younger, there were times in my life that I did not think I was going to make it. Truth be told, another young lady wanted to take my life (literally) over a boy! I was not aware of her plans until after the fact. She wanted to take me out on school grounds; however, a teacher (who was kind to me) heard about her plans and had her removed from school grounds. That was God. That was the Angel of the Lord assigned to me, protecting me and watching over me. It is amazing the things you will never speak out loud to another person but when the time comes for you to be transparent because you are led by God; because you have a testimony, your life experiences must be shared for others to heal. As I said, there were times when I was younger that I did not think I was going to make it. I was not a bad child or a bad kid or a bad teenager. I had opinions. I did not hang around the wrong people or crowd. I just went through some changes. I just went through some things. There were many times I did not love myself. Many times I allowed myself to be used and abused because I was numb to it all. Even as I write these words in my autobiography, memories flood back like ocean waves with tears flowing from my eyes and running down my cheeks. I remember being a kid and my promise to God due to the destructive family life which caused my hurt, abuse and pain. I said:

> *"God if you allow me to*
> *survive and get out of*
> *this, I will not look back. I*
> *will not come back to this*
> *hellhole."*

Some family members may not remember my life the same way I do. But that is OK. Sometimes we mask our hurt and we remember a different reality that was sweeter and kinder so we do not have to face the monsters when we close our eyes. I faced those monsters for many years. Then one day, I did not have to face them anymore. I grew up. I grew out. I kept my word to God. I kept my promise. I did not return to that hell. I just found another.

Fast-forwarding many, many years, I stand before you a broken yet confidently repaired vessel by God. I declare and decree that I am:

- God's servant
- a Woman of God with multiple spiritual gifts (even some untapped into at this time)
- a Pastor (and have held many other positions in the church)
- a Spiritual Mentor
- a Godly Counselor and Consultant
- CEO and Founder of International H.O.P.E. Inc. and my own consulting and publishing company called The Crown And Cross Publishing Co LLC
- one of the many faces on the front cover of the Black Business Directory 2019/2020
- an author of several self-published books
- a woman God used to break the generational curses on my Mother's side by not only graduating High School but graduating without

kids. I was the 1st on my Mom's side to go to college. I obtained my Associate's degree and much later graduated from a well-known University obtaining my Bachelor's degree with honors.

- a Godmother to several
- God called me a Mother to many children who needed and still need love as well as calling me a Scroll

I am God's **CAPAP**: **C**hosen, **A**nointed, **P**urposed, **A**ppointed and **P**ositioned (*the title of forthcoming published work*) to do His will and not my own. Be on the look-out for sermons, workshops, conferences and seminars on this philosophy.

There is another song and I am not sure who the original author is that says "I am free. Praise the Lord I am free. I am no longer bound. No more chains holding me". Some may say this is a funeral song but I beg to differ. When you have been through the fire, able to rise like the Phoenix that God has called you to be, can pray for those who call themselves your enemies, pray for those who despitefully have used and tried to use you, fasted and prayed to ward off witchcraft that people have tried to speak and have spoken over your life, remained quiet to allow God to fight your battles with those who tried to turn friends and family against you and said all ill and improper things about you; have survived some of the worst names called to you by not only family but by friends and those who you thought were close to you; had people lie to your face that call themselves a friend of God; still hold your head up high and cry out to the Lord because you know that He knows the truth; having to be unapologetic for the woman of God that you are and that He has called you to be; even trying to prosper godly business relationships with people that it turns out are not so godly but profess to know and have a relationship with Christ and having saints of God jump up in your face and it is nothing but the Spirit of God that allows you to remain calm and still maintain your composure and peace because you are a new creature in Christ! I always say that I have not been through as much as some but I have been through more than others and I thank God I do not look like what I have been through. With God as my anchor, head of my life and my all in all, I can truly sing "I am free. I am no longer bound. No more chains holding me". That is exactly what I am. Praise the Lord I am free. This book is about me narrating my story. There are no conversations, dialog and very few quotes. These words are written through my eyes, ears and heartbreak while trying to find myself in this journey called life.

Yet Will I Serve Him

Lessons – Part 1

1. Who took God's money

He was calling my phone one late afternoon.

From previous calls over the last several months, since his friend seemed to be preoccupied with other things and they were not "thick as thieves" like they usually were – I would get the calls. I knew exactly what the main three topics he potentially would be calling about: 1. the revolving door of the saints straddling the fence and their behavior; 2. assistance with a project or explaining his tardiness while I taught class due to his other engagement(s) and/or 3. he finally figured out that the collection of church money seemed to get lighter and lighter once it was officially recorded and out of my hands. As I continued to look at the caller ID, a very small part of me wanted to hear the ranting about the members because I was tired of having a meeting about a meeting that had nothing to do with me. I was and still am a firm believer that if certain people break the rules or are caught popping, locking and dropping it at an out of state nightclub or choose to wear clothes with their breasts hanging out or surf the internet for men while traveling to other states and/or are too sick from such activities to come to the House of God, do not involve me. I do not want to hear about it. It was not me and frankly, I am tired of having meetings or discussions about situations that should be spoken directly to said parties. I found out later why a few of those individual conversations could not take place. Once the exposer (person A) exposes someone (person B), that person's sin (person B) is exposed. However, the exposer's (person A's) sin is vulnerable and open to being exposed by potentially B, C, D and so forth. To make it plain, person B's sin will not be exposed because person B will then – at some point – get upset or mad at person A; expose person A's sin, leave and no longer will pay a large sum of "tithes" to person A directly versus paying said tithes to the House of God (I hope you caught all of that – it was a lot).

I do not get into gossip. I only know the facts that come straight from the horses' mouths and there are a lot of horses in these scenarios. A very important life lesson I was taught was that if someone brings a bone to you, what are they taking back to tell others? It is a slippery slope. When it gets slippery, I find it best to bring all of the parties together and the one who refuses to meet, or are too busy to meet or does not want to show up for a meeting, that is the person you should be very leery of.

Now back to the phone call that I finally answered. He was talking so fast I had to tell him to slow down. He asked his question but again between rantings. In the middle of another ranting, I heard – "who took God's money"? I was a little confused and wanted to make sure I did not bring any bones nor take bones. The question was repeated and this time he added more information. Apparently, he had been doing his own calculations and when he added up the finances – since I was out ministering a few times and was absent – he compared the financial books to his own figures and realized that for months, money was off track. Due to him holding a position, I felt that I was cheating him, God and the saints by not speaking up when asked a direct question. I was always taught that if someone asks you a question you must be honest. Plus, I did not call him, he called me. Therefore, I explained that IOU's (I Owe You's) were placed in the offering and it was told to me that certain individuals had paid for certain things and that IOU was to be placed in the books; hence, why the money was off and did not add up. He then said the finances were short by a few hundred dollars and I heard the light bulb go off in his head when he realized the only person I would accept an IOU from – his friend. I explained that I did as I was told. In my mind I was thinking, are **YOU** finally catching on? Clearly when people say they are broke; yet can pay for **YOU** and everyone else for lunch/dinner (excluding me and mine because we do not go anywhere without paying for ourselves), why are **YOU** now looking suspicious? **YOU** were not looking suspicious when the waiter passed by **YOU** and gave the bills to your friend. **YOU** simply wiped your mouth and commented on how good the food was (in case it slipped by, **YOU** was him). He was quiet and then finally – being convicted by the Holy Spirit – said that he knew. He knew in his spirit something was off and not right. The new clothes, the shopping, constantly eating out weekdays and weekends (with him) and the boxed clothing being door delivered, etc.. I had wondered for some time that if all of this happened in front of us, what was going on when we were not around? I simply asked him where he thought all of the spending money and luxury items were coming from. He could not even muster up a response but I already knew that he knew. Clearly, this was a case of "out of sight, out of mind". He regained his thoughts, added a few comments about the saints and said he will be addressing the matter with his friend. A few days later when I overheard the discussion of lunch, his friend (later referred to as the at-fault party) advised that he should pay his own way. I guess they had a conversation after all and it did not work in his favor.

Within days, I addressed the financial issues with the friend (aka the at-fault party) as well as a few other side conversations that were taking place that the saints were not privy to. I expressed that lying to the saints (omitting any truth) was not good and not of God. My pleas were outnumbered two (him and the at-fault party) to one (me). A short time later, God commanded me to not put another cent into that House. I guess God was trying to see if the wisdom He allowed me to speak fell on deaf ears or not. It did. The House was no longer God's. It was the opposite of good ground (also known as good soil) and I was not to invest in it any longer. I did as God instructed and was never questioned. Not too long after, God had me write my first letter of concern and still my words fell on deaf ears. Then it got worse. Due to the constant mishandling of the finances, legal action was going to be brought against all those who held any financial position or connection to the finances. What started off as a small speck of sand was now transforming into a giant avalanche; yet I refused to be taken down. Even though it seemed it was out of our hands and still fell on their deaf ears; I went to the one who could speak on my behalf - God. I thank God that Romans 8:28 rings truth because if it had not, this would have been a whole different type of story. I had to explain my role and the very limited role of another party (who had legal counsel for us on standby) in this financial fiasco in order to get us cleared of any and all wrongdoing and scandal. I had to pay a small fee to have our names removed. Thankfully I had enough funds and I was ok with the fee because it was either pay the minute fee now and seek reimbursement from the at-fault party in small claims court or have a black eye on my record due to the at-fault party's laziness and selfish behavior (who by the way provided an alternate address so that the mail that was intended to come to them was returned). If I went that route, court papers would have been served at my place of employment. No thank you. I choose option one but would not seek any legal action for reimbursement from the at-fault party because you cannot get blood from a turnip. I trusted and praised God that He did not allow the sister I spoke up for and I to suffer any consequences due to the at-fault party's negligence.

Even through all of that, I still remained until God released me. I had to. God still watched and protected me. He was fine-tuning my ears, heart and intentions for Him. Would I serve man or God? Would I listen to His voice? NO MATTER WHAT! Yes. I would. It was no longer about the at-fault party or anyone else. It was now between me and

God. He asked if I trusted Him and I said yes; simply crying — not kicking and screaming. I will not lie, I was crying because I wanted to have a little revenge of my own but what purpose would that had served? I would be no better than the at-fault party. I would be just as corrupt in the mind and heart as the at-fault party. That is what separated us. I had been through worse. This little charade of lies and betrayal was not going to break me. Did it hurt that it was a person who claimed to love God, served Him and His people? Absolutely. Did it hurt because the at-fault party claimed to be my friend? Absolutely but I guess I was more of a friend. Did it hurt when God said separate? No. I had time to heal while in the storm and I had the seeds of bitterness removed and planted with seeds of love, forgiveness and prayer. I diligently prayed for the at-fault party and their friend for over a year and a few months after the fact. Even when I was called in Florida and advised how these two were "talking about" me, slandering my name and trying to decapitate my spirit by spreading vicious, hurtful and hateful rumors about me, I still prayed. There were many reasons for their ungodly behavior, but mainly it was the spirit of jealously. Then one day, I released them back to God. My work was done.

To understand how I was mistreated much worse in life; to understand how this situation was not going to break me and how I came to that place of forgiveness; let's start from the beginning.

2. Let's start from the beginning

$\mathcal{I}$always rooted for the underdog – even if that underdog was me. I was never bullied nor did I bully anyone. I stood up for injustice no matter who was being bullied. As a preteen, I remember once being thrown in the thorn bushes by a boy I liked because I did not want him picking on a younger boy who was my friend. Throughout my life, I always had friends and strangers from school that had issues going on, come to my house. In my eyes, I knew my Mom was superwoman and I wanted to be just like her (but as she said – be a better version). My Mom could fix anything and any problem. If the least she could do was cook them food and listen, then so be it. The person always felt better after a good home-cooked meal and a good ear.

Here are a few examples of situations that tried to break me. I learned at an early age the devil had it out for me. My umbilical cord was wrapped around my neck in my Mom's womb. Little care of knowledge and medicine for young Black/African American teens had me literally born while unraveling the cord from my neck. I survived that attack and grew. In high school, the devil tried to influence a girl to bring a gun to school and shoot me. Apparently, her friends set me up with her boyfriend – unbeknownst to me – and after I hooked up with him, she came to school the following week to kill me. A teacher crossed paths first and ushered me to safety and her off school grounds. Also when I was in high school, I worked in a retail store. An older woman – who was a bully – was talking smack about me. Now mind you, I did not start but in this case, I was glad to finish it. She ran her mouth all day and into the evening until we were about to leave for the night. I just told her that as soon as the door opened to relieve us, I was going to beat her down. The other employees who heard her rantings about me all day oooh'd and ahhh'd. The manager said he was calling the cops. The door opened. The crowd cheered and she ran. I almost fainted from laughing so hard. She called off for a week or so in order to not cross my path. Again, so many things happened in my life that I cannot tell it all: I was sucker-punched over a boy playing a man who was sleeping with several girls. I dated guys who were not the kind to take home to Mom. I drank and drove. I clubbed. I street raced some guys and won. I was an adventurous girl in a small town with small dreams and small minds. I knew that was not the life for me. Not that I am bragging by no means. I am saying that God had my life in His hands even when I was not aware, was in sin and when He was the furthest from my mind.

Intentionally blank page

Family

3. God. Please help me

First, let me say that there is not enough room in this book to tell you all about my experiences with my family and the categories I place them in. But here is the list: my core and inner circle family consists of my Mom, grandmom Theresa and me. My family (the ones closest to me consists of my cousin Tish and my entire family in Philly) and lastly, my family consists of all the others not listed. Outside of this chapter, I will go into even more details in part 2 of my autobiography.

My Dad, you may ask? He is in a category by himself. When I was a child, there were many adult things that my Mom explained to me (i.e. why my Dad was not around, why I needed to go to the Courthouse to prove my Dad was my Dad and why my Mom had to struggle so much if he just lived a few cities over -- in the same state as us -- and so forth). I will say that my Mom never spoke ill of my Dad to me or in front of me. Even in explaining the adult things, her voice was kind toward him; yet, I could see the sign of pain and tears in her eyes. That was one of my early gifts from God - the Gift of Discernment and how to read people. It took a lot of years later to know that gift, understand that gift and why others were intimidated by this gift my Mom and I both shared. I must say that over the years (after I turned 18), my Dad and I have had a much better relationship. We talk on the phone at times but we mostly text which is convenient because he is right there sending me a good morning or good afternoon or checking on me in the evening or just simply saying he loves me. I am glad he is in my life and a part of my life. In the past, we had to have some hard talks and he had to answer very difficult questions but answered them nonetheless. He has been my rock on a few occasions and I am very grateful. My Dad's wife on the other hand was very cold and harsh in the beginning when we first met and many years later. I remember writing my Dad in my twenties (when I was living in Philadelphia) and sometimes my letters would come back - opened - but no response. Odd. Then one day she was bold enough to write me a disturbing letter about keeping my distance from my Dad and etc. Not because I did anything wrong but because of her own insecurities. I have a younger sister (born to another woman) and I am the eldest. So I am not sure if my sister and her mom felt the same frostiness. My Mom felt no need to communicate with my Dad after I turned 18. She thought my Dad and I could work out our own relationship. His wife always felt my Mom wanted my Dad back but that was so far from the truth. Again, when I was under 18, my Mom only called my Dad about me and only reached out about me even when my Dad was unresponsive. Trust me, my Mom seldom called my Dad and instead of forcing him to be a Dad, she just made up her mind to be all that I needed. I will say that years later, my Dad's wife and I did form a better relationship where I felt enough to send her a few Mother's Day cards out of respect but that was short-lived. Somethings are just not meant to be. I will go into even more details in part 2 of my autobiography.

The breakdown of the family categories.

My family: (my inner circle). My Mom, my grandmom (aka Mom-Mom) Theresa and I were the core. I always felt it was the three of us against the world since we were treated as the Black Sheep of the family. We were many times treated as castaways and after a while, you started to feel that in your heart and think it was true in your mind. It seemed like the three of us were adopted into our family. Mom-Mom (my grandmom Theresa) didn't look anything like her mother or her siblings. Yes, you could say that was because she had a different father (as did the others) but she was different. My grandmom was very light-skinned and had beautiful brownish-black moles under her eyes (similar to mine but hers were more distinct). She had the most beautiful long black hair (until her Mother intentionally threw a cast iron frying pan at her head and caused a severe scar around the age of 16 -- more details in part 2 in regards to that horrible and life-shattering situation). Due to the scar being right in the front of her head/hairline, my grandmom had to find creative ways to wear her hair even until death to keep people from asking what happened.

A little back story - my grandmom raised me a few months after I was born until I was about 5 or 6 years old. My Mom was a teenager when she had birthed me and my grandmom felt that she and my Pop-Pop could provide a more stable home until my Mom was able and ready. As a kid, I remember combing my grandmom's hair, greasing her scalp and her teaching me about life: how to keep a house clean, how to scrub a white tub with Comet, how to laugh, play cards and cooking. I remember once when I was a little older, maybe 7 or 8 years old. I wanted to show my Mom and grandmom that I remembered how to cook neck bones the way they taught me. I did everything right and everyone was so proud that I had cooked an entire meal until the neck bones started to boil and there were bubbles forming. Prior to cooking the food, I had to wash the pots I was going to use. Apparently, I had forgotten to rinse out the pots after I washed them hence the soapy water. We ate them anyway and they were the best cleaned and best-tasting neck bones ever!

My grandmom was kind, loving and at my ripe young age of 13, my grandmom had a heart attack and was taken from us. I could not cry at the funeral. I do not remember what she looked like in her casket because I just remembered her smile. I know she is proud of who I have become. My Mom (due to her own teenage rebellion at times) with the combination of family jealousy, secrets (which destroy a family, not bring it together) and constant unnecessary upheaval by other family members caused a huge crack in my Mom and my grandmom's relationship. It seemed that as the time came closer to her death, my Mom and grandmom seemed to patch up the broken pieces. If they had more time, I am certain they would have fully rekindled.

My family: My cousin Tish (who has since passed) and my entire family in Philly were the ones closest to me. They all kept me grounded and I love them so much. It was only when I was with this set of my family that I felt like I actually belonged. Sure I had tons of cousins that I was close to when I was a kid. I still have pictures of my cousin Derrick and me at my birthday parties and him being right by my side every year. I have very fond childhood memories of my great uncle's children and the kids his wife had prior to their marriage as well as all of my cousins. As I said, if it wasn't for my cousin Tish (who has since passed) and my entire family in Philly, I would have not have had any thoughts of belonging.

My family: (all others). My great grandmom D, all of her kids (my great uncle and great aunts) and swarms of other cousins are in this category. There is so much to share from this group. I had some good memories do not get me wrong but when the bad memories and nightmares overshadow the good ones, well that is all you can remember - the pain, hurt and many times feeling unloved and left out by this group.

Good memories: I have warmhearted memories of my one great aunt always taking us to church. She introduced me to God, Christ and Sunday School. I would love when she ushered in her all-white or when she sang in the choir or when she treated me to McDonald's or Don's Dairy for their hot French fries because my other cousins did not feel like going that Sunday or have anything to do with going to services during the week. Also in the summer, we all would visit our family in Philadelphia and I really loved that but hated to say goodbye when the time came. Another great memory was the holidays and the food that was prepared. You thought the movie Soul Food had something on their Sunday meals! We had triple that on Christmas and Thanksgiving holidays. It seemed like food was prepared and everyone had several things they could enjoy. No one was not happy. And the desserts! Oh my! The desserts! Better than any cooking show on TV and better than anyone around the world. I promise you.

Bad memories: seeing one of my great aunts get beat up by her boyfriend, seeing another great aunt get so mad at her boyfriend (which was not unusual) and chasing him around the yard throwing actual bricks at him and family rivalry between one another only to bring outsiders into it. Destruction of relationships is what this group is known for and they may not admit it but it was voiced by all that the helm of the issues was the matriarch herself – great grandmom D. I never speak ill of the dead. I just speak the truth when asked. That's the problem with many African American/Black communities. We hide things so well and will lie to cover up the lie. We will sweep the truth right under the rug even if it involves child rape, the many abortions, STD's, cheating marriages and shacking up, disowning children, the late-night creeping and then it all makes sense when one turns up pregnant; the lies about which man fathered which child, hands always out and never giving back; whose name was on what property and then mysteriously signed by another, bank accounts in various names that just happened to disappear, life insurance policies were taken out by "someone" and you did not even know there was a policy on you; crooked deals were done in the home, liquor sales, shifty-eyed ogling men purchasing liquor and beer at various hours of the day and night, and; heaven forbid you attempted to obtain an education or try to make something better of yourself, you would be shunned. But that is how it was for the "Black Sheep". It was not until many years later that I researched and found out that my last name Stratton is the birth name of the Delawarean family. The other name I was raised to hear was the one they were married into. It is hard being a kid and not knowing or even being told why your last name, your Mom's and grandmom's last names were Stratton and everyone else had a totally different name. Kids teased. Cousins teased and at times, even though the adults knew the truth and never explained it, they seemed to like and enjoyed the frat like hazing.

Years later, after my grandmom Theresa passed, I went from living in a home and riding horses whenever I wanted with my grandmom Theresa and her husband (aka Pop-Pop) to sleeping on the floor of my great grandmom D's bedroom. If we had too many of my cousins and me staying over, her favorite would sleep in the bed with her and I slept on the floor of the windy living room. It seemed like that room could hold heat in the day and could hold nothing but air and cold wind at night. But the thin layered blanket and either my arm pillow or at times a physical pillow kept me comfortable. There was no time for sleep anyway. It was early to rise to clean nick-knacks, sweep and vacuum floors and anything else the adults made you do on the weekends. Do not get me wrong. I did not mind cleaning. It was the excessive cleaning that got my cheeks warm.

I remember a bush that grew tiny yellow flowers on it and when my great grandmom felt you needed punishment for whatever she said, someone else said you said, an adult twisted the truth about you, etc., she was the punisher and used this bush. The bushes grew long, tiny and thin like branches that we called "switches". We would get hit with those switches and anything else that was close to the punisher. We were hit with the switches, the back of great grandmom's hand, a flip flop (or house shoe) or whatever else was close by. More times than not these whippings taught the others to fear. For me, it taught me to hate.

The more you did not cry, the more you were hit or whipped. Later on, I refused to cry and I was whipped just to prove a point. When you cried it was a sign of weakness and it showed the others to stay in line and suffer in silence. Not me. Tears may have made this group feel stronger but I was not giving them satisfaction. My hate grew into a fury of anger. Going to school with belt whipping bruises, lashes from the switches and such hurt when you wore clothes on that area of the bruised skin and especially when it came to bath time. Have you ever been whipped and then given a bath? OUCH! The hot water hit the punctures and whelps in your skin that was left behind and burned. It felt like pouring salt on a wound; it just did not feel good and made you want to cry out but no one was listening. These whippings and mistreatments (honestly it was child abuse but we just did not call it that back then) took place when my Mom worked - which was a lot. She had bills to pay, on time rent to pay to my great gandmom, clothes to buy and a roof she was saving to put over our heads. I remember one night at the laundry mat, one of my other cousins was on laundry duty with me and I despised going with her because she always poked fun at things and others got into trouble. They just said she was special but trust she just liked to poke fun. Anyway, she poked fun at some clothes (underwear) and I tried to stop her and in the process of chasing her with the underwear, I finally got it out of her hand and laughed because I won. Well, I was punched (not slapped but punched) so hard in the front teeth that my front teeth bit my lip, busted it and it was swollen for hours. My Mom was so furious but we were at the mercy of my great grandmom's house and living on the street was not an option. But I learned that if "family" pushes and abuses you mentally, physically and emotionally, the streets looked pretty good and so we went. Strangers treated us better than family.

Violence, abuse and pain were large portions of my childhood that God healed me from. Anger is something He is still working on. Not anger with people. It's just that certain things set me off and I feel like incinerating everything in my path like Jean Grey from the X-Men. Considering, my anger has gotten much better. I try so hard at being mindful to allow the Spirit of God to calm me and keep me calm.

Many years later, God had me forgive my family for every transgression that was done against me because He said that how can they give love and show love when they never even were loved or shown love? That hit me! Even in my twenty-something drunker stooper it hit me, woke me up and I acted as God directed. I came to my senses to realize that their version of love was twisted. It consisted of abuse and pain. How could I expect these family members who physically, emotionally and mentally abused me when the same was done to them and to the generation before and the generation before and etc.? God used me to break this generational curse and then some. For a long time, I did not want kids because I was so afraid that that kind of hideous evil would spill from me, seep into my womb and damage my unborn baby. A very wise friend of mine once said (and I have her permission to use this) that generational curses continue when toxic family members are ALLOWED to continue poisoning the bloodline. Well, my bloodline has been transfused and saturated with the blood of Jesus. Curses are dead in my bloodline. Again, this section will be talked about at length in part 2 of my autobiography.

Intentionally blank page

Friends

4. Living la vida loca (living the crazy life)

You cannot pick your family but you can pick your friends. My circle is so small it is a period. Yes, I have 980 Facebook followers and counting (which is nothing compared to some); however, how many of those people can you message or reach out to or contact and ask to borrow money, help you out of a bind or even borrow a cup of sugar? How about borrowing their car? Not many, I am sure. Again, my circle is so small it is a period and I am ok with that. I do not need 980 friends. I am quite content with my circle and I am not in the market for new friends. I do not need an entourage in order to have people to pray for. I pray for strangers every day and I do not need to know what they need prayer for, God knows. I am just an intercessor. Yes, I have several people I am close to and a handful that are actually friends – many fall into the associate category – but I will tell you that I have one best friend and her name is Nadia. Prior to her, I had a few best friends from school and around the way but we lost contact or they moved out of state prior to me and once I relocated out of state, we just lost touch. I have a sisterly love for them and to this day, two of them reach out from time to time and I am glad they remember me.

Over 27 years ago (when I was roughly 16ish) Nadia and I met and to be honest, I do not know who we met through. It was friends of a friend of a friend and we were all handing out and names were exchanged. Clearly, we are no longer friends with those individuals. People drift never to be heard from again - not us. I am so thankful to her, her family and her kids who are my three beautiful godchildren. 99.9% of the time, Nadia and I agree. She has been and still is my rock. Of all of the things I have done in life, and I have done some pretty wild things, she is my witness. As I type this, I can recall memories of the wild times we had. In my teens, we not only worked next door to one another but at one point, we actually worked for the same retail company in Delaware. She can tell you about the grown woman who wanted to fight me but ran. She also can tell you about the times when: a guy wanted to date me and thought he had game until I had him pay for my lay-a-way (that was the thing when I was a teen) at one store, then had him come with me to her job and made several purchases. His card declined and I asked him for his other one, dropped him off back at home; then she and I went out. I learned quickly that I did not have to sleep with anyone to get things from them (clothes, shoes, jewelry, meals – hey a girl had to eat, right). Or how about the time, this same guy had a friend and wanted to meet

Nadia and I do not know what happened but he went from talking Black to talking like the Lucky Charms man! And the times we went clubbing! I had no problem dancing by myself (of course there were guys who wanted to dance but I had to show off my fly new clothes and I wanted everyone to see me slow grinding the air to Aaliyah's One In A Million. It was so funny because afterward, I had the boys and the men lined up trying to get my number). As Martin Lawrence says – I was a wild boy! Now do not get me wrong, I was not an angel by any means. I just was adventurous and liked to have good fun. I was not a tease either. Back then, game recognized game that's all. Over the years, I met a lot of great gals and guys who made my life interesting and I theirs. I would not trade those memories and experiences for nothing. Yeah, there were times of heartbreak but they kept me on my toes and helped me laugh and SMILE when life threw LIMES (rearrange the word limes into the word smile). There are a lot of things I can remember but I need to scale back on.

I could not end this chapter without a shout out to my best guy friend, my boy Wayne P. in Philly. I have had only two best guy friends in my life. Wayne was one and Bob was the other. Friends for life no matter what!

Love

---

5. Delaware

What can I say about my first love? Even if I told you, do you believe in first love or even soul mates? How about love at first sight? Well, I do to all of the above. At a very young age, I met my soul mate. I cannot describe who was around, where I was at or anything of that nature. Trust me, this was not a little girl having a crush on an older boy (he was only 2 years older) but in the times we were living in, my emotions made me in the eyes of my family a fast little girl. But I was not fast, not infatuated or feeling lustful. I just knew that as soon as our eyes connected, it was like his soul touched mine. Even at such a young age, I could feel an instant lifetime bond between us. It felt as if we had spent lifetimes together. At that time, it seemed like we were meant to be together forever because I would see him everywhere I went – on the school bus, in school, after school and hanging out around the way. I could not get him out of my mind no matter how hard I tried. He was even in my dreams. Apparently, I was not the only girl who thought they were not able to get him out of their minds. He was very handsome, had a different kind of swag and well-liked. The boys respected him. The girls just adored him and he liked them back. Like I said he was very handsome even at a young age.

As time went on, he grew even more handsome and grew into an even more attractive man. A few years flew and I was no longer than flat-chested little girl with fanaticizing eyes but I was blossoming into a young lady. He noticed me again and again but I learned from those other girls. When they "put out", he lost interest or strung them along. He had this charisma that was undeniable and it seemed that no matter how at times he was harsh to them verbally or simply ignored them, they wanted more. So, that was the game he wanted to play – I thought to myself. Well, I am game. It took several years later before he and I had sex and man was it worth the wait! Sex is different with someone you love (like a husband and wife kind of love) versus when you are soul mates. It is just different. Obviously, love is there for both situations (hopefully). But it hits different for soul mates. It was like we reached the cosmic each and every time – even years after our first sexual encounter. There was such a rhythm and flow that made it feel like we were (excuse the expression) in the heavenly. So you can only imagine years later when I heard that he was in a major accident, I almost lost it and I had to go and see him.

I made a special trip to Delaware under the guise to visit my family but to make sure I saw him with my own eyes. People were calling me and telling me so many different stories about what happened, his injuries and that he almost lost his life! I had to see him and hear it from him myself. When I went to visit him at his Mom's house, I had so many emotions stirring inside of me. It had been years since we had last seen one another because after I graduated high school and attended a few semesters at the local community college, I relocated to Philadelphia, Pa. I had heard he was residing in Maryland with his children and his "wifey's" children but who really knew. There were so many women and so many stories I just failed to keep up with. He appeared to have become very secretive after I left and we lost contact but here and there we would reach out to one another over the phone. I never discussed the other women for several reasons: 1. I was not his woman 2. He was not my man 3. My mentality back then was it is all about me. Those time when we did reconnect over the phone, it was love chats and flirty words that neither one of us knew would be fulfilled. Sometimes I think he just liked the fact that the fire was still there between us. We often talked about being soul mates and how it just never seemed to work out with us being in the same state and single at the same time.

So the time came and I was outside his Mom's house and hugged his sister. When he was told that I was there to see him, I was curious how he would look, if he even wanted to see me and other random thoughts scurried across my mind. He yelled from the back that he was dressed for company. The bedroom door opened and our eyes met. It was an atomic bomb of emotions and sexual desire. We both felt it. He invited me to sit down next to him on the bed and he said I did not have to be afraid. Me, afraid? Boy, if it was not for the frail way you were looking, I would have disrespected your mama's house, had sex with you – making you say my name – and wanting to relocate with a sister to Pennsylvania. We chatted, talked, touched hands, reminisced and then we addressed the elephant in the room – his accident. I was not surprised by his honesty and his version of the events since the news, the community and everyone else had an opinion. I was just glad he was alive and I said as much. As our visit ended, I said farewell and his kiss sent an electric current through my entire body. I almost felt like relocating back to Delaware but my life in Philly was great and I did not want to throw that away for a possibility and one exotic; yet memorable kiss. I did not see him for a long time after that.

Many years later, we reconnected over the phone (it seemed like someone we each knew saw the other and decided to "pass" our phone numbers to one another) but it was not the same. I was different. I was growing. I wanted more out of life but I just did not know exactly what that was but I knew it was not what we were doing. I had to end our flirty pleasantries because at some point, one just grows up. At some point, you say to yourself – he is your soul mate but that does not mean that you are meant to be together. Yes, you have these great cosmic sexual experiences and great conversations; yet that is not enough to sustain you. At some point, you just want more than the flirty phone calls and texts throughout the day and night. At some point, you want to hold him forever, make love every day – multiple times a day – and give each other pleasures beyond this world. Your soul may be attached but your heart says it knows him; his flirty ways, his roaming eyes, his unfaithfulness and his quiet times. You know him so well; you know how he moves in those silent times and you are not happy with his movement. Then at some point, you come to the reality that things will never be; it is not meant to be and why force it. I had come to the realization that I was worth more and needed so much more (a lesson I reminded myself often). My future self told the then me that I did not want to be a name on a piece of paper with his last name; to be married and bound by that piece of paper because his body would be somewhere else. He is a roamer and no matter how much time passed, he would be him and is that the life I wanted? My future self was right and that was God really talking to me – even in my sin. I cried so hard that day when this realization hit me. I cried and it felt like the earth cried with me. It rained for days on end during my grieving time. Talk about soul ties! It felt as if someone had literally ripped the very soul from my body and left me there; an empty shell with no comfort, no love and nothing but time to heal. For days, I could not eat, could not sleep and could not work. At times, I laid in bed; then on the couch and back and forth. I cried in each non-sleep position. Eventually, I got in the shower and let the soothing water help cry out the rest of my tears. I dried off, got dressed and did my hair. I got myself together and just took it hour by hour. As time went on, I cried but just a little bit less. Time truly does heal all.

I cannot say that we have not been in touch these last few years but it is different. There is no soul tie joining us. There is no should have, could have, would have any more. Yes, I still believe that he is my soul mate (many may not agree but remember this is not about you or your opinion). I also believe that you only have one soul mate and it does not mean you are meant to be together. God has my future husband assigned to me and I wait with patience and grace. I thank God for His deliverance. The very limited times a year that he and I may chat (or that I choose to respond), it is just good to know that he is still alive and living life.

Intentionally blank page

6. Philadelphia, PA

What can I say about Philadelphia (aka Philly)? Can I tell you I had some of the BEST years of my life there! Can I tell you that I truly did all that I wanted: clubbing, drinking, dancing, bar hopping, the after hour, after hour club spots, dating, white linen parties, Dave and Busters, the pier, downtown nightlife, the Greek Fest, paying for one movie and making it a whole day of sneaking into other movies, eating cheesesteaks (and trust me, the BEST cheesesteak comes from the hole in the wall. The kind of place that is scared of being robbed and you have to order through several inches thick, almost bulletproof plexiglass; big enough to slip your hand through and a side door for your food to be passed through) and the best shrimp off Roosevelt Boulevard! Can I tell you I also had heartbreak in Philly as well?

I will just start from the beginning. I have family (even to this day) that lives in Philadelphia, PA and I can recall over the years in my youth, we would visit a handful of times there (usually funerals). In the process, I became very close to two of my cousins that I met – they were sisters. My Mom was really close to their Mom. I just loved Philly: the houses piled on top of one another, the corner stores that sold everything from a-z, the Chinese food places on almost every block, the hair stores and salons, getting my hair braided by the African women and the excitement. The excitement was everywhere - some good and some not so good. I heard gunshots before in Delaware but Philly was on a whole different level.

Let's go back a little in time – prior to me moving to Philly. At one point after high school and going into my first semester of college, I told my Mom I was bored with Delaware and I wanted to go visit places – anywhere – but I was done with Delaware. My Mom spoke to my cousin's Mom and into the following year, plans were made for me to visit them for a week or so. Let's just say, I had so much fun when I did my initial visit to Philly! I never knew there were clubs you could go to in the daytime and party! My cousin's friends were nice and I felt like I belonged for the first time in a long time. I felt like I had finally found my roots and even though I was younger than them, no one treated me like a kid or a little sibling they had to babysit. I was living my life and it felt good. The men in Philly – woohoo! My cousin's Mom told me to be careful because "these city boys know you are not from here and they will try and use you." Shoot! My cousin's Mom just did not know, I may have been a country girl but I had a city heart. My thoughts: the same way I used my curvy ways in high school with a few fools in Delaware for clothes, jewelry, gas money and dining out, paying my lay-a-way and shoe shopping, it would be the same here. I learned real quick that you do not have to sleep with boys or men to get things. Trust me. I played some and I got played. It was how the game worked then. Again that was my mentality back then. Let's just say that prior to all of this, when I was in high school, it came with its own set of issues and life lessons. Going into my twenties, I was just done with that old stomping ground in Delaware; it was time for some new grazing.

During my week visit in Philly, I actually found a job – customer service. My cousin and I caught the bus back to Delaware so that I could pick up my car, clothes, kiss my Mom goodbye and start my new life living with my cousin (her sister stayed in her own place). My Mom was sad but happy at the same time. She wanted me to experience life and travel and it was a short drive if she needed to come and rescue her baby. I moved to Philadelphia when I was roughly nineteen or twenty years old. I learned the city and would just fill up the gas tank and drive for hours learning every nook and cranny Philly had to offer. North and South Philly I was told to not go to because of the roughness but I did not listen. I saw it all. Thank God He had His hands protecting this rebellious yet free-spirited woman. My cousin and I lived in Northeast Philly in her house and West Philly was and still is where my cousin's Mom lives. I loved both areas.

Skipping ahead in time, my cousin was looking for her long lost brother. She located him through various means and eventually we met up with him and he brought two friends along (unbeknownst to us) but I get it – it was Philly. Trust had to be earned. We had such a fun time together! We laughed, joked and I could not help but notice the one friend. He was so chocolate fine, baldhead, smooth talk and I eventually learned – velvety kisses. He was a hustler and always on his grind. He had MC Lyte's "Ruffneck" down to a science in his own way. There were some things in the song, he was not about. To name a few, he definitely did not have a mouth full of gold teeth (even though that was my thang). He also did not have an attitude but he had this look like "you do not want to mess with me because I can hold my own". He was respectful, observant and I was determined to make him mine.

I cannot say how long after we met that we linked up. He had this witty humor about him and was very intelligent. We could talk about any and everything because he was always feeding his mind by reading anything he could get his hands on. We had so much in common and yet we grew up very differently. When we first started having sex, it was like a booty call but we were not calling on other people to satisfy our needs. I knew he worked in the day and when the night came, he was hustling with various ideas he had. It was about survival. He had him and his crew and really just him when it came to paying his own bills. So I saw him when I could. There were times he would call to check on me and there were times he would come over and stay awhile. For me, it did not matter when he called; I was always available and ready. I loved hearing his voice and loved even more seeing his smile — which he did not do very often. As time went on and we saw more and more of each other, he slowly lowered his guard. He slowly and cautiously allowed me to be a part of his world and his visits were more and more frequent. His life experiences taught him that he could only rely on himself and I dare to say that prior to me if he had been in love with someone, it was not like what we had. I know people say that but I could tell from how cautious he was with his love for me — it was uncharted. We did not say the words (love) but it did not need to be said. Again, this was all new and neither of us had any obligations to each other. We were young, vibrant and both hungering for life and all it had to offer. What made things even better for me was that he did not have any kids. Man, Baby Mama Drama (BMD) was something I was not trying to be in. Life was simple. I have so many memories of him. I remember one night having a conversation and he asked about my plans for that evening. I said the girls (which included my cousin and some friends) were going out. He asked where and I named the place. I knew he was not interested because they had a strict no Tim's (Timberland boots) policy. We agreed that I would hit him up when I got home. Later that night, my girls and I were hanging in the club, drinking, dancing and having harmless fun. Trust me when I say that another philosophy I had was "just because you buy me a few drinks, does not mean you will be getting any". I put that out there from glass one but some men just never learned. They thought that the more drinks I had, the easier it would be. Ha! Wrong! I could drink with the best of them and held my liquor. Remember that I am a country girl so I had practice with various types of liquors, moonshine, Jack, E&J, Boones (yes, even Boones) and beer (which after one sip, I knew that was not for me). My favorite was doing shots. I loved rum and vodka (separate or together – it did not matter). Vodka was always in my freezer and I always had liquor in my apartment cabinets. The cost of drinks was no joke and I was not always so fortunate to have someone purchase my drinks so if a man did not purchase them, my girls and I purchased a round for one another.

At the club, we had several drinks and in most of the Philly clubs we went to, they had waitresses walk around with various types of drinks: shots, tall drinks, short drinks, the flavor of the month and so forth. We hit the waitress up multiple times; sometimes two drinks at a time and I was feeling good. When a guy asked me to dance – which I loved to dance – I said yes. I very seldom said no. My body may have been dancing but my mind was on my man. I was so ready to leave but it was girls' night out. Little did I know that the girls were ready to go too. The second song started playing and my cousin called out to me (I was only dancing a few feet from them) and said my Boo was there. I thought she was joking. When I turned around, there he was coming through the door. You would have thought that I had a warrant for my arrest and the police were after me as quickly as I dropped the guy I was dancing with and swiftly walked over to my Boo (my cousin and I several years later laughed about this). He was with his people and I kissed him as if he had been away for years and we just saw one another for the first time. His lips were so velvety smooth. I looked at his feet and he said he knew the bouncer and he let them in. My man was resourceful. At that moment, we all left. From the blurred memories I recall and my cousin having a lot of laughs at my expense retelling me the story, this is what transpired. I was the passenger in my cousin's vehicle and he was a passenger in his friend's car. At some point, just for kicks, they were honking for us to pull over and we did. All of the drunk people got out and were just acting like fools in the street and apparently, I walked to my man's side of the car and tried "picking him up" like we were role-playing (the funny thing is that we did that a lot – role-playing). All I can say is that we were spontaneous. The great thing is that no one could say they saw either one of us with another person. We all knew. He was my man and I was his girl. That night, we were all dropped off at our respective places. He and I could barely make it up to my apartment steps due to fondling one another. We went from that wild and crazy club sex to making love until the next morning. We dated for a little while longer and started to get serious. I believe we would have eventually have had "the talk" about our future and our plans and the "M" word (marriage). Then one day it was gone. I am not sure what happened. In my opinion, I think that night it scared him to be that close to someone especially when your whole life's mantra was "it's all about me". Now there is the possibility of a full time, this is not just my Boo but my wife (and not wifey). There was some miscommunication and it was not until many years later (ten to fifteen years later) did we talk about the miscommunication and we chalked it up to being young and not addressing our feelings like "adults" should have. I will not lie — two years after that conversation, I wondered about the should have, could have and would have but God did not have Philly in His plans for me. Even then, God was steering my path and protecting me while I was in my sin. God had bigger plans for me and not to say that this guy was not a good plan. It was just that God saw our paths and the right person he would send for each of us.

Lessons – Part 2

7. Supervisors/Managers

God knows I have had my share of overbearing, passive-aggressive, bullying, vengeful, micromanaging, think-I-want-their-job, interview me and value and respect my skills just to turn around – realize how good I really am – and start to nick pick at every little minute thing. I am so over the secular world and looking forward to doing ministry full time when God has released me. The below events from my life will not name names or companies and especially not dates to protect the guilty ones.

Can you believe that with one manipulative and micromanaging manager, I submitted a very lengthy; five-page report and the person sent it back to me because I forgot two things in said report. The first was not capitalizing the letter "T" at the beginning of **one** sentence by the third page into the report. The other was not adding the period (.) at the end of that said sentence! I kid you not, that was all I forgot. I resubmitted the report with the two corrections and the report was approved. This little tennis match – completely unjustified – went back and forth on many occasions. I am not sure why or how it started. For some reason insecure, non-working managers think I want their job and target me. Never do I ever say that I want their job, imply I want their job, ask to learn their job or anything of that nature. Their insecurity and my diligent work make them look bad. I truly believe that the unsaved and those who lip-synch profession of Christ see the light, the God in me; they get irritated because they can find no fault in me or my work. I come to work early (at least 15-20 minutes), stay late and even work weekends and holidays if need be. It appears that my supervisors/managers question themselves (and after how they treat people, rightfully so).

Another supervisor, at a different company, did not like the fact that I walked past their desk one day from lunch and did not speak to them. Please understand that the way their desk was set up, you literally had to walk into their office in order to see their face. However, this person had it out for me and verbally made it known to me. They had checked the time I left to see when I would arrive back (I was always punctual with lunch as well). Since they were so tall, they could see over their wall. Unbeknownst to me at the time, they quietly followed me all the way to my desk. When they were right up on my backside, I had turned to enter my assigned desk. Of course, this startled me and they felt satisfied and walked away. That was it. No conversation. No, I am sorry and no words were spoken; however, there were witnesses. No one spoke up on my behalf regarding the numerous times and the ways I was mistreated. I learned very early in the workforce that it was and is rare for coworkers to see and speak on any injustices they see first-hand.

At one employer, I was told by a new employee that I barely was hired. I was curious why since my resume more than suited the position, I was definitely qualified, interviewed very well (per the hiring supervisor) and I was given a tour of the facility when other applicants were not. I was advised by the new employee (who became a very reliable and trustworthy source) that the color of my skin did not coincide with the existing employees (managers, administrators, etc.) and when the new employee was asked by the hiring supervisor if she felt the same, she replied no because I was very pleasant and was told that my resume outshined the other applicants so "why not hire her"? I was again used to being the only black and many times the only woman in my place of employment, on the team I was hired for and usually – depending on the size – the only Black/African American or person of color in that particular office/branch.

A few years later, I remember working for a well-known company and was asked what I wanted to do next with my time there. Clearly, I was on the path of promotion (my numbers spoke for themselves as well as the performance evaluations and accolades from various coworkers and other supervisors in my department). I began to share an idea to learn other skills in another department (as a side note: never share your full intentions – you will see that people cannot handle ambition especially unsupportive managers). After I shared an idea, I was advised that I was so good that my manager did not want to let me go (a direct quote from said manager). They felt that I was an asset to their team and believed there was more I could learn from them but never explained what "more" was. When I questioned this (my mistake), I was advised by said manager that advancement to another unit or department would not be in my best interest and they would personally and purposely sabotage any chance I had. I was shocked for one that this manager would think of me as such as asset when they intentionally went out of their way to make me look incompetent to other members of our team as well as their manager. Two, I was shocked that someone would allow such words to come from their mouth but let's be real; it was only the two of us in the room – no witnesses. Three, I was shocked because if I was such a bad and incompetent member of the team, wouldn't you try and get rid of me the first chance you could? Later that same week, I was pulled to the side by another manager who had wanted me to assist in training for their team. This manager said that my manager would not allow me to train members of their team and it was simply because I was not a team player. Of course, this puzzled the manager. They saw my work ethic, assisting others, coming in early, leaving late and always smiling in the process (our team was positioned near their team) and they never saw anything but team player written all over me. Eventually, I pursued other avenues in the company to assist with this mistreatment and sad to report, my pleas and evidence were ignored. Witnesses were afraid of the ramifications of losing their job or worse deportation. God said clearly to let go and leave; so I did.

Many years prior to that, I started a new job and so enjoyed the supervisor I had interviewed with only to start the job and was told that she was having health issues and another supervisor was stepping in. Well, there went my sunshine. I was so looking forward to "resting" and not harassment. I was told this replacement supervisor was a very unhappy, recently divorced person who was stuck with the short end of the settlement and was taking it out on everyone. The great day came and it was time for me to be roasted. Well, let's just say that I had come from a prior bad work environment, took two weeks off prior to starting this new job to reset my head only to walk into this. Not today. Not anymore. I played it cool and allowed the supervisor enough room to be the big bad wolf. She did play the role very well – to the tee – and without disappointment. One day, when she came to my desk, lowered her face a few feet from mine and got into my face, I was ready. I inched closer to her face, closing in the gap. I clenched my teeth and with a crazy look in my eyes, I told her that today was not the day. I quietly and softly advised her that if she ever came stomping in my direction again with this bullying persona of hers; I would put an end to it. I told her that I left hell and had no intentions of going back and the same way I walked into that front door, is the same way I would walk out with her in tow. Class over! I never had an issue with her from that day forward and we worked together for several years after that.

At the same company, after being reassigned to another unit to help out and equalize their work volume since I had mastered my current role, I was handed over to a supervisor who many said did not like women. They did not like women in a supervisor role; smart women, educated women, mothers, women of color, women in general. They thought women were only useful in the kitchen – their words. They just did not like women. Well, with said pre-warning, I kept my head low, was friendly, did my job, avoided any complaints from my clients and then it happened. A few customers wanted to send me kudos for great customer service. At first, I received kudos on printed paper from my reassigned supervisor. Then they simply told me to print them myself (and provided the link) because they were receiving too many awards and kudos for me. Coworker compliments started flooding in too and my supervisor just looked in my direction and gave me a nod. I made it a point to never show too much enthusiasm. Time goes on and I have been in this new unit for almost a year and things were good and I managed to stay under the radar. Then a special occasion arose and gifts were given to the team at work by the supervisor (I was out of the office unexpectedly that day). Someone had called and alerted me. What! (I said internally and my supervisor's actions shocked and perplexed me. A snake never changes. It always slithers on its belly). I was told that everyone's face was shining bright when they were presented with their gift by our supervisor. The next day I had returned to work and thought that my turn was coming. All-day long and nothing. There was no shiny box or beautiful wrapping paper or even a verbal compliment for me. For over a year, I had worked hard and assisted this team to bring their closing numbers up and intake volume down. I was given nothing. When the team inquired, apparently there was a grave error in counting and the supervisor assured everyone – including me – that the error would be corrected immediately. I wondered how long immediately was because to date, I am still waiting on said gift.

I have so many personal testimonies to share but I will end this section with this last one. Years later in my industry, I wanted to train new hires because I knew how it felt to be new, handle a diverse workload with no training and expected to sink – but instead thank God - I swam. I also was (and still am) exceptional at my job. My performance, work evaluations and kudos portray this. Early in my career at one particular job, I created a training manual, put together a presentation and had the full support of my new supervisor, friends and loved ones. I gave an overwhelming 15-minute presentation and blew the socks off the training team, my supervisor and management. After a bunch of red tape and months later, I was finally given the opportunity with the backing of my supervisor. The company sent in ten new hires and gave me full control. Little did I know that they (training team and management – not my supervisor) wanted me to fail. They came in at intervals, sat in on the various trainings and were reviewing my sessions. Unbeknownst to me, their intentions were to unanimously fail my sessions and use that against me to never train again; hoping to crush my dreams in the process. Well, what the devil meant for evil, God turned it around for His good. Their plan backfired. One of the Training Team Members had a change of heart. As the Training Team Member sat in my various sessions apparently the member grew a conscious and realized that not only was I great at training but my shoes would be hard to fill (the Team Member's words). When asked in front of me, after all of the training had ended, the Lead Manager thought their Training Team Member was going to still go with their plan and give me a bad review. Instead, the Training Team Member spoke so highly of me that I was almost in tears. This proves that you do not have to say a mumbling word. The battle belongs to the Lord. God will make your enemies your footstool. The Lead Manager was so furious that the Training Team Member was asked to leave the room. On the way out, the Training Team Member gave me a wink and said I did a great job and to add insult to the Lead Manager's injury, the Training Team Member made sure to compliment me by adding that no one could do a great job as I did – not even the Training Team Member! In the end, the Lead Manager did not offer me the training position; which was also rejected by the Training Team Member who gave me the rave review. The position went back to Corporate – out of state.

My point to this portion of my life story is that I always wanted to know what recourse do employees have against these types of supervisors/managers/leaders that I mentioned above? Human Resources? Laughing so loudly. No. In my experience, Human Resources has the interest of the company at heart – not the employee. The answer is God.

One small piece of advice: if a friend offers you a position under them and they will be the supervisor, RUN! It is not a good idea. You will soon learn their bad habits and behavior while at the same time wonder how they are still in their position?

To end this chapter on a good note, I can say in my entire career I have had two good-natured and good-hearted supervisors. The first is when I worked at a clothing store as a teen. She was one of the most understanding and awesome managers there. The people liked her and to this day, I pray nothing but blessings over her life. The second was my supervisor I met many years later. He was (and I am sure he still is) a very kind, generous and fair family man. I know his family loves him. I saw it in his sister's eyes (they worked together and I believe they still do). He has no idea how influential and bearable he made my life and on occasions, I did tell him the same. I thank God for him every day and pray blessings in his life also.

Remember this book is called – *Yet Will I Serve Him*. Even in the midst of all of this (and you were only provided with a snippet of my life); yet, I still served Christ and still continue to serve Him to this day.

Preview:
Yet Will I Serve Him
The Sequel

Yet Will I Serve Him

The Sequel

Have you ever felt like your breaking point was coming? You can feel it. You can sense it. You know that the very next thing someone does or says will tick you off to the point of no return and then it is blackout. You know that you are going to be so caught up in the essence of the matter at hand, that by the time they finish their sentence, you either put your hands on them, or some non-Christian words are going to come out of your mouth or both. Here's my story.

"Hey you guys," I called out to the Ladies group that I was going to be working with for the day outside the church building. It seemed like only two of us were always doing what we needed to do but the others just dragged their unwilling selves just because leadership asked them to. There was no we in team and the two of us (we) were doing all of the work. This prompted me to call out to the others and that is when it all went downhill.

I was confronted by one of the women who had an ungodly spirit attach itself to her that very moment. As Christians, we know we are constantly in spiritual warfare and that when God is blessing, the enemy is always messing. The ungodly spirit in this woman caused her to step outside of her "normal" self and approach me in a very confrontational manner. I would not have believed it if I was not there to witness it. As she made hand gestures directly in my face to express her dislike of me calling out to them, my flesh started to rise. I did not say anything disrespectful. I became inflamed in my body, but my spirit was as cool as a cucumber! While standing directly in my face, hand gestures and all, she continued to carry on. I could feel her breathe on my face and the "old man" in me (that God cleansed me from) was about to rise because we do live in this flesh. I gave my life back to the Lord a little over a year prior but let me tell you, this had been a very trying year. God was still working on this vessel and some things He had not finished working on – my anger was one of them. As usual, it lay just below the surface and all that I had been going through with this ministry and God's people was just about all I was going to take. My anger had nails clawing on my inside like freshly sharp knives to get out and show her that she definitely did not know who she was messing with. This ministry only saw the "nice" Sister Kim. I never knew walking through these halls would be so difficult to bear. No one wanted to see the other side. Heck, I did not either which is why I was trying to be calm. A part of me wanted to physically put my hands on her, pound her face on the sidewalk and show her that taking my kindness for weakness was a huge mistake. In the midst of her babbling (which was all I heard) and my anger, the entire world became dark and all I could see were the colors red and orange. I could visualize this entire beat down that I felt I had to give her, but then I heard the voice of God. It was like God Himself could not even send His angels to talk me out of my head right now because I was too far gone. He had to come down Himself. There was just silence as if I had gone deaf. God reminded me that this woman was someone's Mom. Someone that I had and still have great respect and admiration for. The Spirit of God won the victory over my flesh. The Spirit of God in me stood firm, made eye contact, held my ground, and showed no signs of irritation. The Spirit of God put my flesh under subjection and calmly told her that "this" (all of the attitude and hand waiving she had given) was not of Christ. Somewhere between my cool tone, the Christ-like words that flowed from my mouth, and staring down the ungodly spirit inside of her, it seemed like she had an epiphany. She then stopped dead in her tracks. The Spirit of God moved me to start walking away while still being saved and never losing me. Look at God! Even in the center of it all, He still walks with me. Through my trials and tribulations, and though the enemy tries to slay me, yet, will I serve Him! Yes, I could have let the enemy win the battle and the war, but not so! God's Word reassures us that the battle does not belong to us, but to Him. The Bible says in Zechariah, 4:6 "Not by might nor by power, but by my Spirit."

Just when I thought the showdown was over, then she ……

To Contact The Author

Please write to:

International H.O.P.E. Inc.
Kimberly Stratton
PO Box 952607
Lake Mary, FL 32795
Email: kimberlystrattontheauthor@outlook.com
Website: **kimberlystrattontheauthor.com**

To Get To Know The Author
And Her Works

Please visit: **kimberlystrattontheauthor.com**

Intentionally blank page

Notes

_____

_____

_____

_____

_____

_____

_____

_____

_____

_____

_____

Other Books Written
By The Author

- ➤ A Voice For The Silent Ones
  self-published April 2020

- ➤ It's StoryTime Vol. I ~ Coloring Book
  self-published September 2020

- ➤ It's StoryTime ~ The Journey
  self-published October 2020

- ➤ It's StoryTime ~ The Journey Continues
  self-published October 2020

- ➤ It's StoryTime ~ The Journey Never Ends
  self-published October 2020

Upcoming Book Written
By The Author

- ➤ Yet Will I Serve Him - The Sequel
  to be self-published

About The Author

First and foremost, I give honor to God who is the Head and Captain of my life. Without God, I know exactly where I would have been ~ on my way to hell. Writing this book – as well as the others that are forthcoming – is only the beginning. This has been a tremendous experience that I would not trade for anything in the world. I am so humbled and honored to be a broken yet repaired vessel to be used by God.

I give honor to my Mom – Patty – who has been a rock in my life and a HUGE supporter. It was not popular to be unwed and have a child in the 70's. No matter the trials and tribulations my Mom went through, she did not abort me but LOVED me, cried for me, took care of me and taught me many valuable life lessons that have helped form who I am today. God then took that mold and transformed me to be a Speakerbox for Him.

I was born in Delaware and grew up there as well. After graduating High School, and spending a few semesters at the local college, I heard my heart beating for new life and relocated to Philadelphia, PA with my Mom's blessing. From Delaware to Pennsylvania to Florida, life has been an adventure ever since (and I will write the books to prove it).

Without giving away too much, just know that with all that I have been through, I have allowed no one to steal my joy. I stand before you a Woman of God, dedicated to do His will, in and out of season; whether it is popular or not; received or not. I will continue to stand flat footed and uncompromising on the Word of God. He has called and chosen me to preach and teach His Word locally and abroad. His plans are superior to mine and I accept that God has positioned me for the purpose and plans He has for my life. The best is yet to come.

I also give honor to all those who have loved me, supported me (spiritually, financially, mentally and emotionally), prayed for me, donated to me or my nonprofit International H.O.P.E. Inc., mentored me, celebrated me, honored me as God has spoken and everything in between. So many have invested and spoken blessings and positivity in my life that there are too many to name but they know who they are.

I pray that you continually pray for me, my friends, my family, loved ones and the ministries God has appointed us over as we continue to lift your names before the Lord.

I am also grateful to God for allowing me to set up my very own consulting and publishing company called *The Cross And Crown Publishing Co LLC*. Check out our information on www.kimberlystrattontheauthor.com for more details.